How
Animals Live

by Tristan F. Nicholas

What helps animals live in their habitats?

Animals live in many habitats.
Their body parts help them.
Some animals live in cold habitats.
Fur helps them keep warm.

Living in the Ocean

Shells keep some animals safe.
Some animals have **antennae.**
Antennae are feelers.
Antennae help them smell and
taste too.

Antennae

How do animals get food?

Animals use parts of their bodies to get food.
Birds use beaks to eat food.
Camels store fat in their humps.
They use the fat for food.

Other Ways Animals Get Food

Lions have strong legs.

Lions can run fast.

Lions can catch food.

What can help protect animals?

Camouflage makes an animal or plant hard to see.
Camouflage can be a color or a shape.
Camouflage helps living things stay safe.

Hiding in the Water

The crocodile lives in the water.

It keeps its eyes above the water.

The other animals do not see it.

Animals Warn of Danger

Animals help each other stay safe.
A deer lifts its tail when it is
in danger.
Other deer can see the tail.
They run away to stay safe.

A peacock makes a loud call.
Other peacocks hide to stay safe.

What are some parts of plants?

Plant parts help plants live. **Roots** take in water. Roots hold plants in the ground.

Roots

The **leaf** makes food.
The **flower** makes seeds.
The **stem** moves water in the plant.

Stem

Leaf

Flower

Plants in Different Habitats

Plants grow in many habitats.
Some plants have leaves.
Leaves can be many sizes.
Leaves can be many shapes.

Some leaves look like spines.
Some leaves look like needles.

What helps protect plants?

Spines keep animals away.
Spines help some plants stay safe.
Some plants use camouflage.
Camouflage makes the plants hard to see.

Spine

Plants and animals live in many habitats.

Plants and animals use their parts to help them live.

Plants and animals help each other.

Stone plants

Glossary

antennae feelers that help animals feel, smell, and taste

camouflage a color or shape that makes a living thing hard to see

flower the part of the plant that makes seeds

leaf the part of the plant that makes food

root the part of the plant that takes in water and holds the plant in the ground

stem the part of the plant that moves water to other parts